Common Dolphin
8 feet

Common Porpoise
6 feet

Narwhal
15 feet

Ganges River Dolphin
8 feet

Amazon Dolphin
7 feet

Finback Whale
80 feet

Blue Whale
100 feet

Gray Whale
45 feet

Humpback Whale
50 feet

Whales

Friendly Dolphins and Mighty Giants of the Sea

by Jane Werner Watson • illustrated by Richard Amundsen

GOLDEN PRESS • NEW YORK

Western Publishing Company, Inc. Racine, Wisconsin

ACKNOWLEDGMENT

The author and the publisher wish to thank Dr. Richard G. Van Gelder and Miss Marie A. Lawrence, Department of Mammalogy, The American Museum of Natural History, for their invaluable help in checking the text and the illustrations in this book.

On the cover: (Front) *A Humpback Whale comes up for air. Barnacles like to fasten themselves on the Humpback's bumpy head.* (Back) *A Humpback swims near the surface, blowing out a column of spray through its blowholes.*

CONTENTS

When a whale appeared, men in small boats raced to get close enough to heave their barbed harpoons into its back. Many times the men were tossed into the sea and the boat was dashed to bits by the wounded whale.

What are Whales?

Out of the sea springs a small, sudden fountain of spray and foam. The fountain shoots high into the air, then swiftly dwindles. For a moment a dark shape hovers on the surface of the ocean. Then it too vanishes from sight.

Watchers on the shore—or perhaps on the deck of a ship—call to one another, "A whale! Did you see the whale?"

It is always exciting to see a member of this family of sea dwellers. For the order of **cetaceans**, to use the scientific term, includes the world's largest living animals. Some are as much as 100 feet long!

A hundred years ago, when whales appeared, the call was often, "Thar she blows!" Men on whaling ships raced to throw their sharp, barbed harpoons at the broad, shining backs.

A thousand years ago, a bell from a watchtower on a sea cliff sounded when a whale was sighted. It called all the men of a seaside village to a whale hunt.

We do not know when the first men in small boats went hunting these marvelous creatures, which they called "monsters of the deep." We do know that whales swam the seas at least 60 million years ago. That was many millions of years before the first human beings lived on earth.

The whales that swam the seas millions of years ago included the two main kinds that live today. One group—or suborder—includes all the toothed families that bite their food. The other suborder includes all the whales that strain their food through *baleen,* or whalebone, "sieves" in their mouths.

The principal families with teeth are Sperm Whales, Beaked Whales, Ocean Dolphins, White Whales, and Freshwater Dolphins. The principal families with whalebone strainers in their mouths instead of teeth are the Rorquals, Gray Whales, and Right Whales. We shall become better acquainted with all these families.

We know from fossils that all the principal whale families lived millions of years ago. Fossils, you know, are remains of once-living things, found in rocks. Long, long ago, some whales went aground on beaches or died at sea and were washed ashore. Their bodies were swiftly covered by wind-blown sand that gradually hardened into rock. With the passing of time, their bones turned to rock, too, and became fossils. Scientists can figure out the age of these layers of rock. In that way they can tell how long ago the plants or animals lived whose leaves or shells or bones have turned to stone.

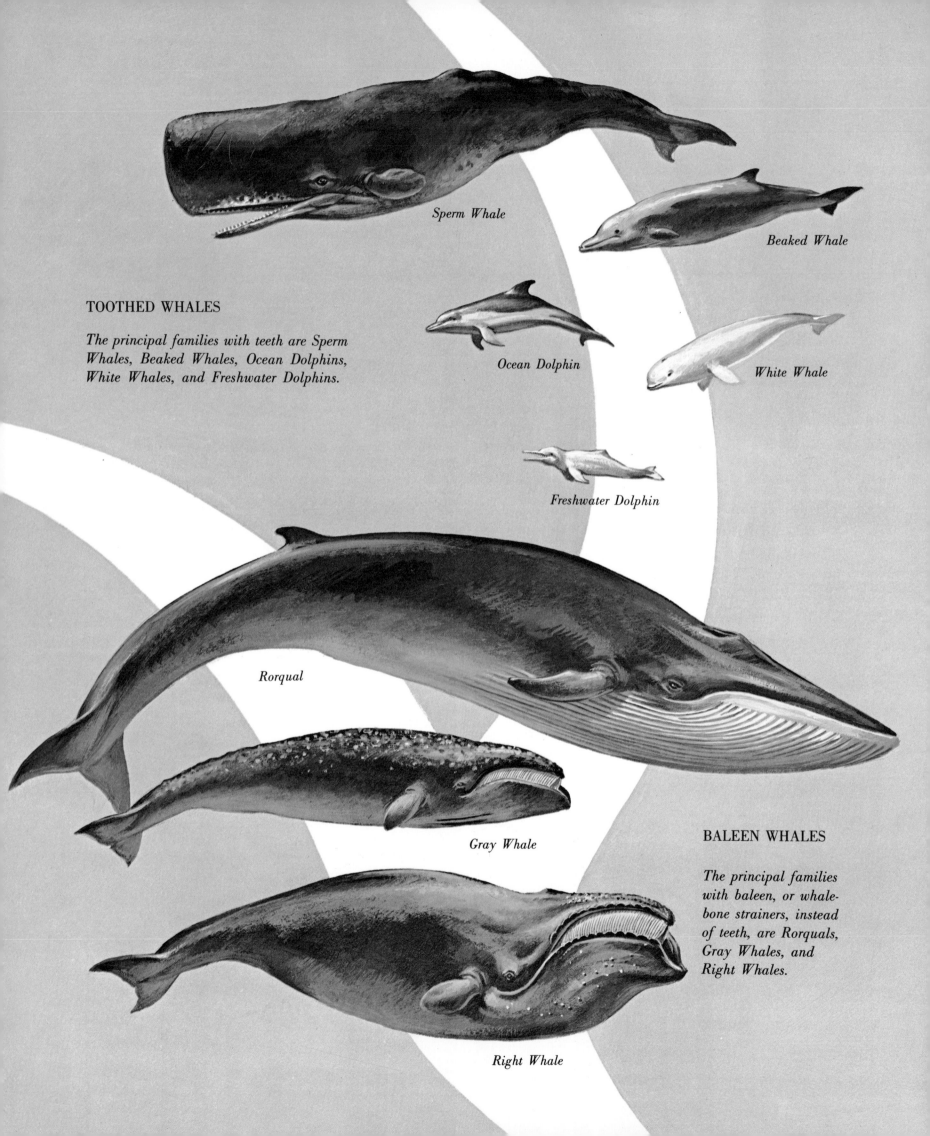

Sperm Whale

Beaked Whale

TOOTHED WHALES

The principal families with teeth are Sperm Whales, Beaked Whales, Ocean Dolphins, White Whales, and Freshwater Dolphins.

Ocean Dolphin

White Whale

Freshwater Dolphin

Rorqual

Gray Whale

BALEEN WHALES

The principal families with baleen, or whale-bone strainers, instead of teeth, are Rorquals, Gray Whales, and Right Whales.

Right Whale

The last common ancestor of both the toothed and the whalebone whales probably lived about 65 million years ago. After that, the two varieties began to develop along separate paths. This kind of change and development is called evolution. It is a process that goes on very, very slowly all the time, in both plants and animals.

It was probably even more than 65 million years ago that the common ancestors of the two varieties we know today left the land to live in the sea. For today's giants of the sea are not fish, who have always lived there. They are not reptiles, like those long-ago giants of the land, the dinosaurs. Whales, dolphins, and porpoises are mammals.

Mammals are warm-blooded, often quite intelligent animals. Mammals breathe air into lungs. Almost all mammals give birth to live babies instead of laying eggs, as fish and reptiles do. Mammal babies feed on their mothers' milk. And usually mammals have somewhat hairy coats.

The land ancestors of whales probably walked on four short legs, rather like those of the hippopotamus. Perhaps they had hoofs like the hippos and deer and cattle we know today. They probably had furry coats.

But in the long, slow process of adapting to life in the sea, whales changed in many ways.

Whales no longer have fur. When mammals live on land, hair (or fur) helps to hold in their body heat. When they swim in the water, though, hair is a nuisance. It slows their swimming. So, gradually, whales and porpoises and dolphins lost their hair. (So have water-loving hippopotamuses.)

Whale babies often have some hair on their heads and lips and chins. A few keep some whiskers until they are adults. But most whales have thin, smooth skin. Under the skin is a thick, light layer of fat, called *blubber*. Just as hair helps to keep land mammals warm, so this blubber helps to keep the sea giants warm. It also helps to streamline them and to make it easier for them to float.

Smooth skin slips easily through the water. It slips best of all when it covers a smoothly rounded, streamlined body. Whales have changed their shape to become quite streamlined. Their heads have become very large. Often the head is one-quarter to one-third the whole length of the body. The whale's big head swells out smoothly to join its mid-section. There is no trace of a neck between.

The bone structures of the Toothed Whale and the Baleen Whale. One important difference is the shape of the jawbones.

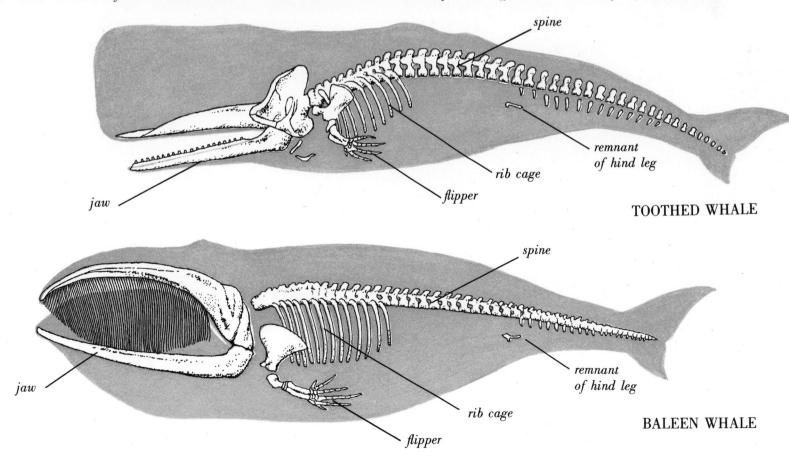

spine

remnant of hind leg

rib cage

flipper

jaw

TOOTHED WHALE

spine

remnant of hind leg

jaw

rib cage

flipper

BALEEN WHALE

The hippopotamus, in water most of the time, breathes oxygen from the air by keeping its nostrils above the waterline.

Fish live entirely underwater. They have special organs called gills that extract oxygen from the water to supply their needs.

The whale lives underwater but comes up to the surface every few minutes to breathe air.

Front legs have changed to flippers or paddles. These are more useful for balancing and steering in the water. But some of the old bones of forelegs, fingers or toes are still there, inside the flippers.

The hind legs of the land-dwellers have disappeared, but some whales still have hind-leg bones hidden inside their bodies.

Probably the ancestors of whales once had long, thin tails. On land, a long, skin-and-bones tail with a tuft of hair at the end is useful. It can flick away insects. In the water, a wide, flat tail is much more practical. A whale's tail is now flat and wide. It has two horizontal sections, called *flukes*. These are very useful in helping the whale to swim swiftly.

Most whales still have three compartments in their stomachs, similar to those of grass-eating animals that live on land. And whales still breathe air into lungs. They need the oxygen in air. Fish need oxygen, too, but fish get oxygen from the water around them. They breathe by taking water in their mouths and passing it over their gills. The gills remove the oxygen from the water. This explains how fish can stay underwater all their lives. Not so with whales, porpoises, and dolphins. They must come to the surface every few minutes to breathe air.

When a whale comes to the surface and blows out a column of foam and spray, it is just breathing out. You breathe out several times every minute. If you dive underwater, you must come up quickly. You cannot safely hold your breath and stay down for more than a minute or two. When you come up, you probably gasp and gulp in air.

The whale's body uses oxygen better than yours does. So a whale can stay down as long as ten minutes. On a deep dive for food, a whale may stay down as long as thirty minutes. Then up it comes to breathe out a cloud of moist, warm, oily air. This turns to steamy vapor as it rises in a tall spout.

The whale's nostrils are in the top of its head. We call them *blowholes*. Whalebone whales have two. Toothed whales have only one usable blowhole.

The whale opens its blowhole and breathes in through it. Then it closes its blowhole and dives. So it never gets water in its "nose." A human being has to be careful about diving very deeply. The weight of all the water above presses down and can crush a person's rib cage. But some people think that what saves the whale—or porpoise or dolphin—from being hurt in a deep dive is that its rib cage is flexible. This bony structure can bend or "give" under a good deal of pressure without being damaged. Others suggest that the whale's layer of blubber acts as a protective shell. Whatever their secret is, some whales can dive down 2,000 feet or more. Their muscles and fat store extra oxygen, so they do not need to breathe so often. And their heartbeats slow down to save oxygen.

At last, though usually after no more than thirty minutes, whales must come shooting up to the surface. They blow out their spray of vapor and breathe in a great series of gasps, as many as fifty times.

If a whale has fed well, it may float for a while at the surface, resting. There it can enjoy the gentle, rolling motion of the waves and the cool breeze over the ocean. It may even doze off for a little nap.

A whale never gets what human beings think of as "a good night's sleep." The thick blanket of fat under its skin is light and helps to keep the whale afloat. But it must make a little effort—a flip of the tail at least—to stay at the surface. If it sank into the water, sound asleep, it might not get to the surface again in time to breathe. And that would mean the end of it.

Having to wake up to breathe is no problem for a whale. Sleeping in little naps is its natural way. Over long, long ages, the whale's body and habits have adapted to life in the water.

Another process that has had to adjust to water living is the birth of whale babies. Water-dwelling reptiles, such as crocodiles and sea turtles, come ashore to lay their eggs. Some water-dwelling mammals, such as seals and walruses give birth to their babies on land. But whale babies, called *calves*, are born in the water.

The baby grows in a special sac inside the mother's body. Like human and other mammal babies,

A baby whale emerges from its mother tailfirst when it is born. A friendly whale usually stands by in case the mother needs help.

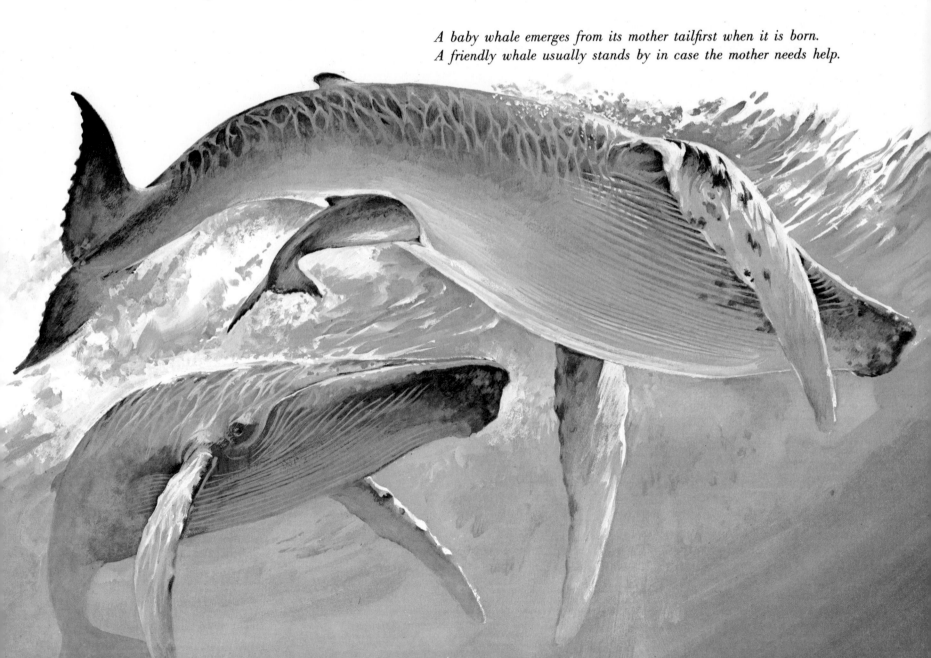

it gets nourishment and air from its mother while it is growing there. Human babies are generally born headfirst; but the whale baby slips slowly out into the sea, tailfirst. This means that the baby's muscles have a little while to get used to working in the sea while it is still breathing through its mother. If it were born headfirst, it might drown before it wriggled free.

A newborn baby whale has to be able to get to the surface to breathe right away. As soon as the baby is born, the mother guides it up to the surface with its flippers. There the baby takes its first breath of air. Friends may gather around to help the mother. A baby whale is very well cared for. Its mother stays close beside it, so that the baby can swim in the shadow of that big comforting body.

When the baby is young, it has a drink of milk every twenty minutes or so. It must take its drink quickly, because it has to go up to the surface every few minutes for a breath of air. When the baby's mouth touches the mother's breast, the mother squirts milk into it. This is an easy way for the baby whale to get its milk. It is quicker than sucking for it as human babies and many other baby mammals do.

In many ways like these, the bodies of whales—including the smaller dolphins and porpoises—have adjusted to life in the sea. This watery world is their true home.

A mother whale guides her new-born baby up to the surface to get its first breath of air. Soon the baby whale will learn to do this by itself and will continue to come up for air every few minutes for the rest of its life.

Whale Talk

The underwater world is as noisy in its way as a city full of human beings and their machines. The water itself sloshes and surges. In the sunlit, blue-green layers close to the surface, small shellfish crackle and snap their crisp outer parts. Larger fish bubble and burble, grunt or puff, as they swish along, fanning their tails. Above the waves, hungry sea birds moan and cry. And around them the wind shrieks or hums.

Whales add to the sea noises. Sometimes they smack the surface of the water with their broad tails —*smack, crack*! The sound is as sharp as a rifle shot.

Most of the sounds we hear travel through the air in waves. But sound travels through the water, too, in unseen waves. Men have found that some of the sounds whales make can travel through the water for hundreds of miles.

Whales often roll and toss at the surface, sending water sloshing loudly about them. They blow spouts of foam that shower down in tinkling droplets. They leap almost straight up, arching their huge bodies through the air. Then they splash down on their sides or backs with a tremendous noise.

There are times, though, when whales just float quietly. They listen to all the sounds around them. And it seems that they understand many of those sounds.

Whales keep in touch with one another and with the world around them mainly by sound. They have no sense of smell. They can see, but not straight ahead of them. Their eyes look out to the sides—one to the right, the other to the left.

Whales do not see color. They do not see the strange, eerie hues that often flash in the water as schools of fanciful fishes swish by. Whales do not see the bright reds, yellows, and purples of sunrise and sunset. Many of them travel far, to the icy waters of the Antarctic and the Arctic. But they are never aware of the glorious curtains of blue and green and gold that shimmer in icy skies. The beauty of the *aurora borealis,* the "northern lights," and the *aurora australis,* the "southern lights," are wasted on whales, just as colors beyond our range of vision are wasted on human beings.

Hearing is much more useful and important to whales than sight. But it is not easy to see a whale's ears. As whales' bodies became more streamlined, their outer ears disappeared almost completely. Only very small holes remain in their place. Whales do hear well, though. Their inner ears, deep inside their heads, are protected by especially thick bones.

It is possible that whales also have special ways of "hearing" through their foreheads and jaws. And they seem to get messages directly from sound waves touching their skin.

Each variety of whale has a special "language" of sounds. Men who have spent years at sea can often identify whale families just from the sound of their breathing. Sometimes they recognize the special rhythm of swishing tails as the whales swim along in family groups or *pods*.

Whales also seem to be able to identify one another by sounds like these, just as we recognize the footsteps of someone we know well.

Whales seem to talk to one another. They do not have vocal cords that vibrate when air comes up from the lungs, as humans do. So their sounds are not just like those of human beings. But whales do make many different sounds. To people who have listened carefully, some whale sounds seem like squeaks and squeals, squawks and hums. Others are like whistles and whines. And some are like rich musical tones.

Some whales give a wild sort of cry when they are unhappy or in trouble. Others "speak" in a language of clicks. Baby whales soon learn to click like the adults. If you could listen to them carefully,

you would find that they take turns in "speaking." Surely they must be carrying on some sort of conversation!

Most whales live together peaceably in large groups. In order to do this, they must be able to exchange signals and information. They have very large and complex brains. We know that they not only can learn to play games but can make up new games. We know that they make friends and play together, and that they seem to miss one another if they are kept apart. We know that they are fond of their families. So it seems likely that they can understand many kinds of messages.

Clearly, a whale can do much more than recognize other families of whales and fishes by their typical sounds. It can also recognize friends and its own family. A mother can call to her baby, and the mother can recognize the baby's voice when it replies. Whales that are mates know each other's voices too, it seems. And there is warm feeling between them.

Some sounds that whales make are too high pitched for human ears to hear. We hear sounds when sound waves vibrate or quiver against our eardrums. The more waves per second, the higher we say the *frequency* is. And the higher the frequency, the higher the pitch. There is a limit to the high, shrill sounds our ears can handle. Some dolphins make sounds that vibrate ten times as fast as a human ear can hear.

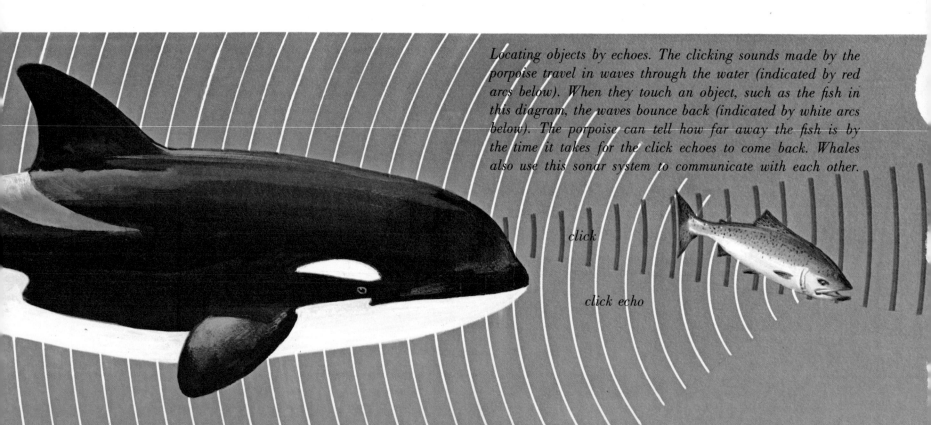

Locating objects by echoes. The clicking sounds made by the porpoise travel in waves through the water (indicated by red arcs below). When they touch an object, such as the fish in this diagram, the waves bounce back (indicated by white arcs below). The porpoise can tell how far away the fish is by the time it takes for the click echoes to come back. Whales also use this sonar system to communicate with each other.

click

click echo

A small Pilot Whale was trained to locate a torpedo on the ocean floor and attach a device that could bring it to the surface.

These small whales are friendly and sociable. They like to swim around boats or near people on beaches. They visit among themselves and make sounds that seem to convey messages.

For a long time, scientists have been trying to understand dolphin "talk." They have to listen with special instruments in order to hear some of the high, superhuman sounds that dolphins make. Using these instruments, they make tapes of many dolphin "conversations." Then they count the number of times certain sounds occur and try to figure out what the different sounds mean. The scientists have made some progress, but so far, no one can really understand the dolphins' language. Do you suppose the dolphins, with their large brains, can understand ours?

Whales, large and small, use a special sound system in hunting for food. We call this system *sonar*. It is a way of locating objects by echoes. Submarines and flying bats as well as whales use sonar.

A whale sends out sound waves. When they touch an object, the waves bounce back. As these reflected waves echo back to the whale, they tell it how large the object is and how far away. If the object is something good to eat, this is very useful to know.

Just how whales send out their sound waves we do not know for certain. Bubbles are sometimes seen rising from the mouths of whales, but these do not seem to be related to sounds. Whales also produce vibrations. These vibrations are called *ketophonation*. This term comes from old Greek words that mean "whale-soundmaking."

Some scientists have managed to make use of whales' sonar. U.S. Navy men worked in one experiment with a Pilot Whale weighing about 1,200 pounds. They trained the small whale (1,200 pounds is very small for a whale) to recover objects from the ocean floor. This is the way they did it.

The men trained the small whale to let them place a yellow rubber bit in its mouth. Down on the sea bottom near by, they dropped a large object. In this experiment, the object they dropped was a torpedo, fitted with a special device that gave off sounds.

The whale learned to swim to the torpedo and clamp the yellow rubber bit onto it. Then the whale swam back to the ship for a reward of fresh fish. The rubber bit had a balloon attached to it with a gas supply. As the balloon filled with gas, it floated to the surface, lifting the torpedo with it. So the navy retrieved its "lost object," thanks to the help of the Pilot Whale.

Men have also found the small whales called porpoises and dolphins helpful in fishing. Fishermen in the Mediterranean, and other seas, too, usually go out at night, with lanterns bouncing at the prows of their small boats.

Most schools of fish, you see, go down into deeper, darker waters by day. It is as if they were avoiding the harsh glitter of the sunlight. But at night, when the waves are softly washed with silver gilt from the light of the moon and stars, the fishes rise from the dark depths. They come close to the sur-face. Sometimes the fishes themselves glow with a fairylike sheen as they streak through the waves. Then the fisherman lower their nets to scoop up their catch.

Dolphins often leap and splash and play near the boats. Fishermen in small boats enjoy having the graceful and friendly dolphins nearby. And sometimes the dolphins swim around a school of fish and drive them into the fishermen's nets. This is a great help to the fishermen.

Once in a while, a dolphin finds itself trapped in the net. The friendly fishermen let it go, of course. And the dolphin gets a good fish dinner for its help.

Commercial fisherman out for tuna in large, swift ships have not been as friendly to dolphins. The tuna fishermen "accidentally" kill as many as 100,000 to 200,000 dolphins in their nets every year.

Friendly dolphins sometimes help fishermen by driving fish into their nets.

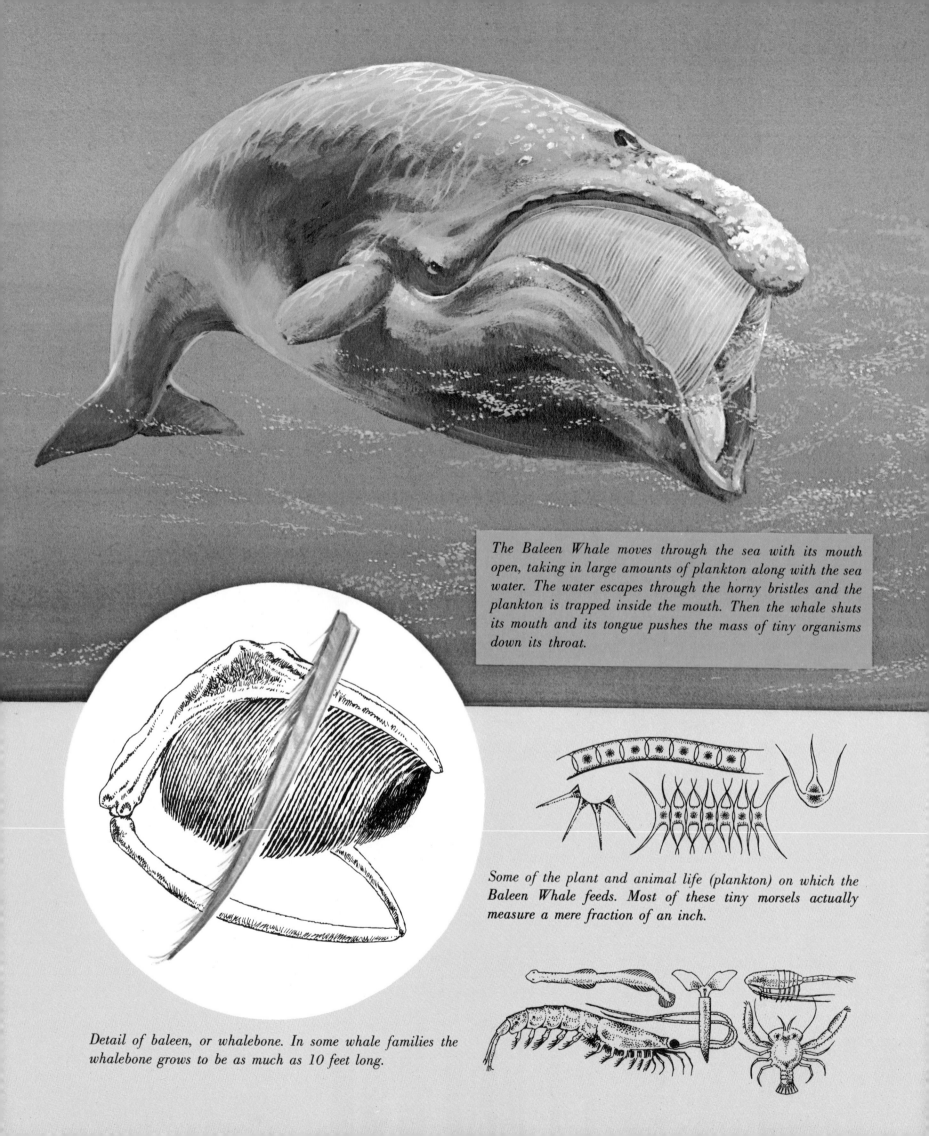

The Baleen Whale moves through the sea with its mouth open, taking in large amounts of plankton along with the sea water. The water escapes through the horny bristles and the plankton is trapped inside the mouth. Then the whale shuts its mouth and its tongue pushes the mass of tiny organisms down its throat.

Some of the plant and animal life (plankton) on which the Baleen Whale feeds. Most of these tiny morsels actually measure a mere fraction of an inch.

Detail of baleen, or whalebone. In some whale families the whalebone grows to be as much as 10 feet long.

ELEPHANT
(12 feet tall, weighs 6 tons)

BLUE WHALE
(100 feet long, weighs 120 tons)

The Blue Whale dwarfs the elephant and even the largest dinosaur known to man. Its head alone weighs 800 pounds, and its huge stomach can hold two tons of food at one time.

DINOSAUR (Brachiosaurus)
(80 feet long, weighed 50 tons)

THE BLUE WHALE

The largest land animal alive today is the elephant. It may stand 12 feet tall and weigh as much as 6 tons. The largest land animal that ever lived was the 50-ton dinosaur called *Brachiosaurus*. But the Blue Whale that still swims the chilly seas dwarfs any elephant. It is larger by far than any dinosaur. It grows to as much as 100 feet in length and can weigh as much as 120 tons. The females grow to be even larger than the males.

Blue Whale is also called Sulfur-Bottom. It is really blue-gray in color. The name Sulfur-Bottom comes from the yellowish film of tiny creatures that sometimes forms on its underside. Like all Whale-bone Whales, it has two blowholes that are closed when it dives and opened when it comes up to breathe and spout. And like all Rorquals, it has grooves on its throat.

Blue Whale's whalebone is black and only about three feet long. Men have found the longer whale-bone of some other varieties of whales more valuable.

In addition to whalebone, the other product for which whales have been hunted is the oil boiled from their blubber. No other whale can match Blue or Sulfur-Bottom for blubber! The thick, fatty, 30-ton blanket under the skin of one giant Blue Whale can be boiled down to provide 70 to 80 barrels of clear oil. Whale hunters were well aware of that fact. So they pursued the Blue Whales until there are hardly any left in the sea.

Blue Whales used to range all the oceans of the world. They could travel, when they chose to hurry, at a speed of up to 15 knots (about 15½ miles) per hour. This is about the speed of a loaded freighter. In winter they could be found in equatorial waters—the warmer stretches of ocean near the equator. In spring and early summer they traveled north to the cold waters of the Arctic or south to the Antarctic.

As recently as 1930, seamen and scientists estimated that there were about 150,000 Blue Whales. By 1960 there were only one to three thousand left. Whalers on huge whaling-factory ships had been killing thousands every year, especially in the Antarctic Ocean, where the largest Blue Whales could be found.

Now the number of Blue Whales left is so small that some scientists think it may already be too late for them to raise families and increase their numbers. In 1972 men of many nations decided to put a stop to whale hunting. So Blue Whales may still have a chance. But you will be lucky indeed if you ever see one of these splendid giants of the sea alive.

23

THE SINGING HUMPBACKS

A strange, mournful cry echoes across the ocean's sun-glinting surface on a clear spring day. People who have heard this sound describe it as something like the moan of a bagpipe with an oboe groaning alongside it. This is the song of the Humpback Whale. Far out at sea, where the shoals of small fishes are plentiful, the Humpbacks are journeying northward.

It is spring, and the young fish are feeding on a host of still smaller beings—tiny sea urchins and snails and shrimp among them. Some of these shellfish float close to the surface for a short time in the spring, when they are very young. Many of them make a meal for a Whalebone Whale.

Some of the Humpbacks are mothers with small calves close beside them. Whenever Mother sends up a spouting fountain, Baby spouts a little two-foot-high column of spray.

Mother darts away now and then for a mouthful of plankton. She closes her mouth on her catch and pushes out the water between her lips with her tongue. She swallows the solid food held back by her whale-bone strainer. Then she flips her tail and hurries back, calling to her baby.

Whale mothers are fond and affectionate. Mother Humpback has a tender way of wrapping her flipper around her baby. She can do this easily, because she has very long, armlike flippers. They are a third as long as her whole 50-foot length.

Humpback Whales are not as handsome as many other whales. They move slowly and clumsily. They are rather bumpily built. And barnacles like to fasten themselves on Humpback's bumpy head, flippers, and 12-foot-wide tail flukes. But to a baby Humpback, its mother looks just right.

The Humpbacks—mothers, fathers, and young—are regular travelers on the ocean highways. Every spring they leave the tropical waters where their babies are born. Those who live north of the equator swim northward. Some hurry along the coast of Scandinavia. By early summer they reach the icy Barents Sea.

Most whales start migrating toward warmer waters in the autumn. But the Humpbacks stay in the Arctic longer than other whales. It is December or early January before they start to head south again. The babies are old enough now to add some mouthfuls of plankton to their diet of rich-mother's milk. On their southward journey, the pods generally swim closer to shore than they did on their way north.

A young Humpback calf is well protected by its mother's long flipper.

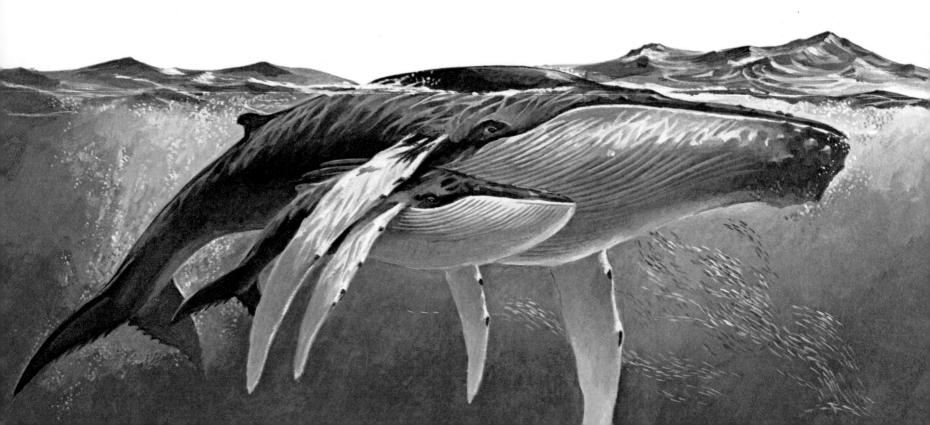

SPEEDY FINBACK

The midnight sun of Arctic midsummer spreads a dusky golden glow over the sea. Under its light, the dark waters of the Bering Sea shine with a cold gleam. Suddenly a sleek black shape appears on the surface. Another rises close by, and another. Soon a dozen 70-foot Finback Whales are playing in the chilly twilight.

Slowly, gracefully, the sleek giants rise from the water. Their huge bulks, gray above and white below, curve smoothly. Then they splash down, sending up huge fountains of spray.

Finback, at 70 to 80 feet, is smaller than its cousin Blue. This difference in size has saved the Finbacks for many years, while hunters pursued the larger Blues. Finback is slimmer, too, but otherwise it is similar in shape to Blue. Like Blue, Finback has one fin rising from the smooth curve of its back.

The right side of Finback's head is lighter in tone than the left. Whalers tell us that the same is true of the whalebone inside its huge mouth. On the left side, the whalebone is gray. On the right side, it is yellowish white. No one knows the reason for this.

When the Finbacks have finished their play, they streak swiftly away, in response to some signal no man can hear. For a few minutes not a sign of a sleek back can be seen. Then black spots appear on the surface again, off in the distance. And spouts of foam rise, pale against the dark water and golden sky.

Perhaps the Finbacks have received a faint echo signal. It may tell them that a dinner of krill—tiny baby fishes and other tasty morsels—is not far away. Whatever the message, off they go.

Finbacks are swift and lively swimmers. Their speed has sometimes been a lifesaver to them. Sinking a harpoon into a swift-moving form is a difficult task. But modern whalers have taken a heavy toll. So there are few Finbacks left today to play under the midnight sun.

BRYDE'S WHALE

SEI WHALE

OTHER "GROOVED THROATS"

If you should see a Sei Whale, it would be hard to tell it from a Finback. The Sei is likely to be somewhat smaller, it is true. A Sei is seldom longer than 60 feet. But that is still a very long whale!

Sei's throat grooves are somewhat shorter than Finback's. But Sei's outstanding feature is inside its mouth. Its whalebone is especially fine and soft and white.

Most Finbacks like northern waters. Most of the Seis seen in recent years have been south of the equator.

If you see a whale in the really warm waters of the Atlantic or the Pacific, it is probably not a Finback or a Sei. Look closely. Does it have a very small dorsal fin on its back? Are there two ridges on the top of its head? When it seems to be standing upright in the water, can you see grooves on its throat? And is it less than 50 feet long? If so, you have had a rare treat. You have probably seen a Bryde's Whale. There are not many of them around to be seen any more.

The smallest of the Rorquals is Minke's Whale. It grows only to 28 or 30 feet. It has so little oil in its coat of blubber that the whalers have left it alone. So there are still many Minkes swimming the seas.

Like their cousins, the Minkes are traveling most of the time. In spring they head north to the rich feeding grounds. The males travel together in the open seas. The cows (female whales) with their young calves stay closer to the coasts.

Usually, when young whales start to travel on their own, they do not go very far north during the first few years. But some Minkes are found in all the oceans of the world.

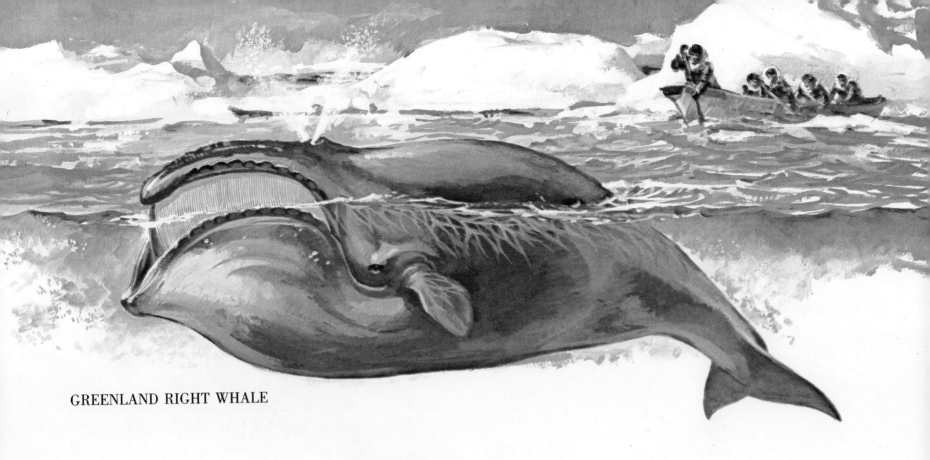

GREENLAND RIGHT WHALE

The Right Whales

A broad stretch of gleaming wet black back rears up above the surface of the icy sea. It is the back of a whale. That is easy enough to tell. But what kind?

As the huge creature rolls gently with the waves, no fin appears, rising from its back. That is one clue. Soon it lifts its great head to peer around. We can see no furrows striping the smooth pale throat. That is another clue to its identity.

The big mouth opens and we catch a glimpse of whalebone hanging like a curtain inside. Now we know that this is a Baleen or Whalebone Whale. Since it has no throat furrows, it cannot be a Rorqual or a Gray Whale. The only other family of Baleens are the Right Whales. We can guess the branch of the family to which this whale belongs from the location of the sighting—as we shall soon learn.

BIG MOUTH, THE BOWHEAD

An iceberg floats close to the Arctic icecap. Under an overhanging shelf, a pair of whales surfaces to "blow." They are 50-foot Greenland Right Whales, also known as Bowheads. Because men have hunted them so relentlessly, not many Bowheads are left today to swim the icy seas.

The reason for the nickname "Bowhead" is easy to see. Imagine a head nearly 20 feet long. It occupies a third of the Greenland Right Whale's vast length and curves up on top to form a high bow, or arch. Inside, Bowhead's mouth rises almost as high as a two-story house. One could never get a clear view of the height of this cavern, though, even by stepping

inside the huge mouth. For it is filled with rows of whalebone that hang down from the top of Bowhead's arched upper jaw. And some of the whalebones hanging from the high center of the arch are as much as 14 feet long! Those that hang from the down-curving sides are shorter but still astonishing in size.

Like most whales, Bowhead is gray above, with a white chin and lower jaw. Like most Right Whales, it does not have a fin on its wide, sloping back. But the plump shape that starts with its big arching head is Bowhead's alone. So chances are that you would recognize a Bowhead if you were lucky enough to see one in northern Pacific waters.

BLACK RIGHT WHALE

A close relative of Bowhead can sometimes be found in the temperate waters of the Atlantic and Pacific. This is Black Right Whale. It may grow to be 55 feet long, with a head one quarter of its length. A horny sort of "bonnet" forms a bump on top of its head. But its mouth is not nearly so large inside as Bowhead's. Black Whale's baleen (whalebone) is only about 7 feet long at most.

Black Whale likes to wander. With its pod, or group, this whale migrates with the changing seasons and the changing food supply. But it does not usually travel as far as the coldest waters of the very far north or the far south.

BLACK RIGHT WHALE

PYGMY RIGHT WHALE

PYGMY RIGHT WHALE

Pygmy Right Whale is a distant cousin of Black. But they rarely meet. Pgymy lives in the southern waters off South America, southern Africa, Australia, and New Zealand.

Pygmy looks a little like its larger relatives among the Right Whales. But Pygmy has a small fin on its back; most other Rights Whales do not.

Pygmy Right Whale does not grow to be more than 20 feet long. It is rarely seen by whalers. But when it is, Pygmy is left more or less in peace, while larger whales have been hunted until they have all but vanished from the seas.

The Long-distance Grays

Gray Whales may grow to be as much as 45 feet in length and have a few rather short furrows on their throats. The few thousands that survive, after years of pursuit by whalers, now travel in the western Pacific, and along the west coast of North America, wintering in sheltered lagoons off Lower California.

One Gray Whale who traveled the waters off North America became famous. This is her story.

WAS IT GIGI?

The boys and girls on the sightseeing launch were having a wonderful day. The Pacific Ocean off the southern California coast was calm under a bright blue February sky. The school group had come to see Gray Whales. And the Grays were putting on a show.

Whale spouts boiled up like small geysers on all sides. There were so many that no one could watch them all.

Some of the whales lifted their great heads high out of the water. The boys and girls could see a few rather short furrows striping the huge throats. And a small eye close to each end of the long, smiling mouth watched the children who were watching the whales.

Suddenly one whale surfaced close beside the launch. After blowing her spout of foam, she did not dive. Instead, she bobbed close to the boat.

"She's smiling at us!" some of the children cried.

"I think she wants to be fed," said a boy.

The whale rose from the water, almost upright, to look at the children in the launch.

"Maybe it's Gigi," someone said.

Gigi! A wave of excitement spread through the crowd. Within seconds, everyone who had a camera rushed to the rail to take a picture. For Gigi was a famous whale.

Marine scientists had caught the baby whale with a tail noose, back in March, 1971. Very likely they lifted the baby in a canvas sling onto a rubber raft, and towed the raft to a waiting vessel.

On this vessel was a big tank. The baby whale was soon splashing around in it. When the ship reached port, the baby was lifted once more in the canvas

sling into a waiting truck. A 16-inch-thick foam-rubber mattress slung in a canvaslike hammock kept her comfortable while she traveled. Fifty gallons of seawater were splashed over her repeatedly to keep her wet, since a whale's skin must be wet at all times. Soon she reached her new home, an aquarium near the coast. There she was given the name Gigi.

Gigi was well cared for. The aquarium was filled with seawater from the ocean that had been her home. Gigi was fed a diet that was as much like her mother's milk as the men could make it. Whale's milk is very rich, so Gigi was fed ten gallons of whipping cream every day. Vitamins, yeast, and other good things were added to the cream. It took four men to feed Gigi, through a stomach tube.

The baby whale gained an average of 26 pounds a day. She weighed 4,325 pounds when she was 11 weeks old. When she was a little more than six months old, the men looking after her knew that she was old enough to start eating solid food. They fed her a mixture of small fish, shellfish, and other small sea animals and plants. This mixture was much like the krill that Whalebone Whales eat at sea. About 180 pounds of the mixture a day kept Gigi happy and well fed.

For a year Gigi lived in the aquarium, while the scientists observed her to learn what they could about whales. But Gigi was still growing rapidly. The men could see that she was soon going to be too large for even a very large tank. As an adult she would be nearly 50 feet long and would weigh about 40 tons. So the scientists decided to set her free.

First they trained Gigi to find her own food. Then she was hoisted out of her tank. She traveled back to the coast by truck.

From the truck, Gigi was transferred to a tank on a U.S. Navy barge. The barge carried her out 15 miles from shore. At last Gigi was allowed to slide down from the tank on the back of the barge, to land with a gigantic splash in the ocean once more.

Gigi was 15 months old, 27 feet long, and weighed about 7 tons when she returned to sea. She wore a small radio sending set fastened to her back. This was to give scientists information about the migrations of Gray Whales. At least they hoped it would.

There were Gray Whales in the waters where Gigi was released. They were traveling north again. Gigi's human friends hoped that she could join a pod—a family group of whales—and travel with them to the Bering Sea. There she would find plenty to eat.

For some weeks, men at lookout points along the Pacific coast reported hearing the "beep" of Gigi's small backpack radio. This cheered her friends. They were sure she was safely on her way.

Then there was silence. From time to time a note appeared in newspapers about Gigi. Once the papers reported that a team of scientists had gone north to hunt for her. Another time a scientist announced that he thought she had stomach trouble. "All those gallons of whipping cream!" he said disapprovingly. But no one had any definite information.

In the autumn, the Gray Whales came south again. People along the Pacific coast began to watch and to listen for Gigi. No one looked for her in the Atlantic. Other varieties of whales are seen there, but the Grays have long since vanished from the Atlantic Ocean.

"It is useless to listen," said a scientist who had worked with Gigi. "The backpack we put on her back was designed to last just six months. That time is up. It didn't work very well anyway."

Could anyone hope to recognize Gigi? She had more than doubled her weight during her first year of life. She would be much larger now. And wouldn't she look just like any other Gray Whale?

"It might be possible to recognize her," people who knew Gigi well said. "She has a distinctive white stripe on her tail."

But no one did recognize Gigi on that southward journey.

For a few months after that the Gray Whales rested. Their winter home is in the sheltered shallow waters off Lower California known as Scammon Lagoon.

A hundred years ago, whaling ships used to wait outside the lagoon. When the Gray Whales swam out to start on their 4,500-mile journey, the hunters pounced. Some used a cruel trick.

Many of the female whales had young calves with them. These calves had grown in their mothers' bodies for a year or more. They had been born in the lagoon. They could not yet swim very rapidly or dodge very well.

The whale hunters knew that a mother whale would not leave her calf. If they harpooned the baby, the mother would stay close and try to protect it. She might lift it on her flippers and try to carry it to safety—even though it was attached to the whaling boat by the long line on the harpoon that had struck it.

Those old-time hunters knew that if they first harpooned a baby, they could easily kill the mother. Whale hunting like this nearly wiped out the Gray Whales. In 1946 there were only about 250 Grays left.

Then laws were passed to protect them from hunters. The Gray Whales increased rapidly. When Gigi was set free in 1972, there were ten or eleven thousand Grays for her to join.

In early 1973, thousands of Grays once again began to pass lookout points on the Pacific coast. Private boats took whale-watching parties out to sea. It was from one of these boats that the school children sighted Gigi. At least they thought they did, white tail stripe and all. She was swimming happily about their boat. She seemed glad to see people again.

Some of the photographs taken that day were shown to people who had known Gigi well. One or two said, "Yes, that's Gigi!" Others were not sure.

The children were confident, though. They liked to think that they had really spotted Gigi that sunny winter day, among hundreds of Gray Whales. And newspaper stories spread the good news. Headlines read: "Gigi Is Alive and Well."

A Sperm Whale will dive as deep as 2,000 feet in search of his favorite meal, the Giant Squid. Along the way he may be stabbed by the long, sharp sword of a 15-foot swordfish.

Whales with Teeth

Many families of whales have teeth. These teeth are covered with ivory that is something like the enamel on human teeth. But there are differences. For one thing, we humans grow small teeth as babies; as our jaws grow, our baby teeth fall out. Then we grow a second, larger set to fit our larger jaws. Whales grow only one set of teeth. Until a young whale is well grown, its teeth remain sunk in its gums. Its jaws and tongue are strong enough to handle soft food in the meantime. When its jaws have grown to full size, its teeth come through. Each year after that, a thin layer of ivory is added to each tooth. By counting the layers, it is possible to guess the age of the whale.

The number of teeth a whale may have differs a good deal from family to family. There is no standard number. Some whales have teeth in both upper and lower jaws. Others have teeth only in the lower jaw. Their teeth are not planned for chewing but only for seizing food. Most whale teeth are large and cone-shaped.

With these teeth a whale can seize a large fish or a slippery squid and hold it fast. Most Toothed Whales feed on fish, so naturally they spend their time in waters where there are plenty of fish to be found. This explains why most Toothed Whales live in moderately cool, or temperate, waters, not very far from shore.

Toothed Whales are generally smaller than Whalebone, or Baleen, Whales. In fact, the only real giant among the Toothed Whales is the Sperm Whale. It may grow to 60 feet in length. Killer Whales may grow to be 30 feet long. But most of the other Toothed Whales— **Odontoceti** is their suborder's scientific name—range from 13 to 20 feet. Dolphins and porpoises are the smallest members of the great order of **cetaceans**, which includes all the whales. These small cousins are mainly in the 6-foot to 12-foot range.

Members of one of the five main families of the Toothed Whales actually live in rivers or sheltered harbors. These are the Freshwater or River Dolphins. The other families are the Ocean Dolphins, the White Whales, the Beaked Whales, and the Sperm Whales. Let us take a closer look first at the Sperm Whales, the giants among whales with teeth.

In the black depths of the sea, a Giant Squid fights fiercely to escape the massive jaws of a Sperm Whale.

Sperm Whale, or Cachalot

Sunlight winks on the waves at the blue-green surface of the sea. But farther down the color deepens. It may darken first to bottle green, then to deep purple. Many schools of fishes spend their days in these dim regions which the sunshine cannot reach. They rise to the surface at night, when the sun is safely out of sight.

Still farther down, blackness spreads over the cold depths of the sea. It is quiet here, too, for few fish live in these waters. Only occasionally does a fish slip past, perhaps flashing a light from its own body. And once in a while, in the wilderness of the ocean 2,000 feet and more beneath the surface, a huge Sperm Whale may appear.

Sperm Whale dives down here from the surface, with a flick of his broad tail and a graceful flip of his huge dark body. As he dives, his heartbeat slows. His blood concentrates in his heart and brain, where it is most needed. He draws upon the reserve stock of oxygen stored in his muscles and in his thick layer of oily blubber.

During the dive, a 15-foot swordfish swims toward Sperm Whale. The long, sharp sword that tips the fish's upper jaw catches Sperm Whale in the shoulder. He swerves in his dive so sharply that the fish's bony sword breaks off. The point of the sword, two feet long, is left sunk deep into Whale's coat of blubber. There it itches and smarts. But Sperm Whale continues his dive.

A slimy brown lamprey fastens itself to Whale and sucks at his blubber with rubbery lips, drawing blood. Whale will not be stopped by a pest like this. With a swing of his tail and a push of his flippers, he continues his dive.

Now Sperm Whale sends out his "feelers" of sound. These sound waves roll out through the water. Soon, deep in his skull, Sperm Whale gets a message. His echo system tells him that a real treat lies ahead and to the left. With a flick of his tail, Sperm Whale glides in that direction.

The treat is a giant squid, the big whale's favorite food. Long ago, squids were shellfish. Gradually, through evolution, they gave up wearing the shells that protected their boneless bodies. Ten long, limber arms flail out around each squid's mouth to feed it. Although many squids' bodies stretch only a few feet across, the arms of some giants reach out as much as 50 or 60 feet.

These giants are the only squids that live in the dark depths of the ocean. They are the largest known animals without backbones. Many grow to weigh 400 pounds. They have been known to weigh as much as a ton.

Sperm Whale's echo system tells him that the squid nearby is a really big one, so Sperm Whale is on guard. He knows the force of those long, waving arms. They are lined with suction cups as large as teacups. These cups have a powerful grip. Even if a squid

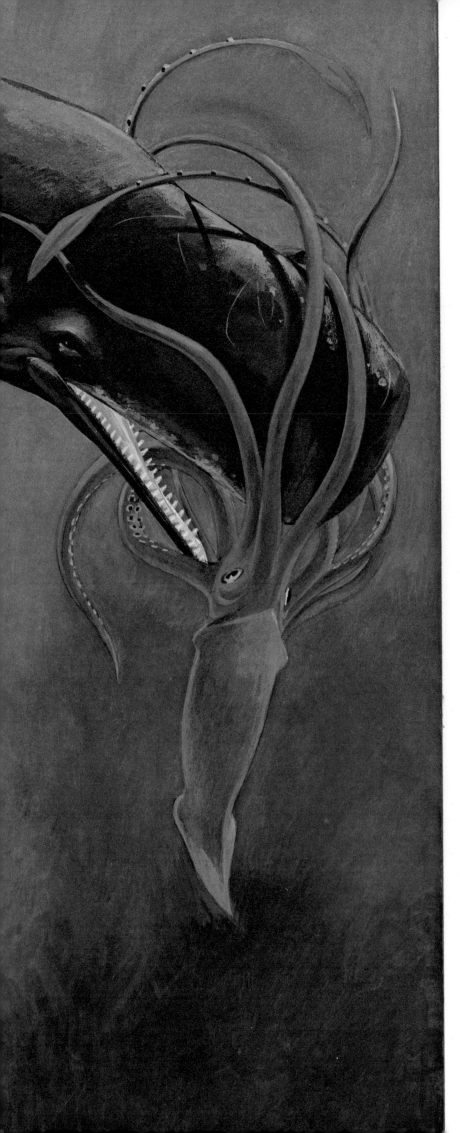

loses the battle, it can leave rows of lasting circular scars on a whale's skin.

Now Squid's huge, 15-inch eyes have spotted Sperm Whale. Squid's long, limber arms begin to flail the water. Whale catches one arm in his sharp-toothed mouth. In a flash, Squid wraps other arms around Sperm Whale's blunt nose and huge jaws. Squid's circular suckers bite into Whale's thin skin.

The waters around them churn into a dark froth. Sounds of the struggle ripple out in every direction. When the uproar clears and quiets, Giant Squid has vanished. Sperm Whale glides away with a satisfied look.

Well fed for the moment, Sperm Whale heads for the surface with a flick of his tail flukes. He is ready for some deep breaths of good sea air.

At the surface, Sperm raises his great, square head high into the air. He blows his low, arching spout—which on clear days can be seen far across the waves. His eyes look to this side and that.

Seeing the broad, finless backs of several members of his pod floating nearby, he drops into the water with a huge smack. Up goes a shower of foam. And out goes the message: The King is back!

Sperm Whale swims over to rejoin his family, and is glad to be back with them. The family includes a few young adults. There are youngsters, of course. And there are the "cows."

Sperm Whale is a powerful old bull. He has a number of wives. That is the way families are arranged among many of the Toothed Whales. (This is the way of sea lions, too.)

The female Sperm Whales, or cows, are smaller than the bulls. They grow to be around 35 feet in length and may weigh about 16 tons. Bulls may be 60 or 65 feet long and weigh up to 60 tons.

The bull whales do not stay with their families all year. The males migrate to the coldest seas in the summer. There they feed on sharks as well as their favorite meal, squids. They also enjoy snacks of smaller fish.

The migrating whales may meet a school of salmon heading for some river mouth. The salmon are bound upstream to lay and fertilize their eggs. Instead, many

of them may end up as a meal for a Sperm Whale. These giant whales may gain a ton of weight in a single summer of feasting in the far north.

Sperm Whales like company, so the bulls often travel north in groups of 200 or so. A few stay in the gloomy northern (or far-southern) seas all year. But most head back to warmer waters for the winter. There they rejoin their cows and youngsters. They set up family living again, and start new babies.

The bulls guard their wives and children well. If danger approaches, they attack. Sharks up to 40 feet in length often follow the whale family. They hope to be able to snatch a slow, weak member of the pod. But if these sharks are wise, they keep an eye out for an angry bull!

A Sperm Whale will even attack a boat, if it feels that its family is threatened. It will shoot up to the surface, raising its snout 10 to 15 feet into the air. Its eyes peer out on both sides, while its tail and flippers move rhythmically to keep it in place. As a warning signal, it often snaps its great jaws, with a fearsome sound.

Then up go Sperm Whale's tail flukes. Its flippers churn. Down it dives. But it is not headed down into deep waters after food this time. Instead, it dives just under the boat, to ram it with its great forehead. Then Whale's huge jaws lock in the wood to rip and tear. Or its broad tail swings around to smack the boat a crushing blow. Many a whaling boat in the old days met its doom in the form of a Sperm Whale.

But Sperm Whale's great claim to fame is not the damage it can do. Its outstanding feature lies in its huge square head. There is a bony case in Sperm Whale's forehead that contains a fine oily and waxy substance, called *spermaceti*. While the whale is alive, the spermaceti is liquid. It is thought that this liquid and its case serve some function when the Sperm Whale dives or makes some of its distinctive groaning sounds.

After the whale is dead, the spermaceti is removed from the skull case by the bucketful. Then the oily liquid hardens into a pale wax. Men have found many uses for this clear, colorless, odorless substance. It was used to make sweet-smelling candles. Later it was used in cosmetics and ointments. The oil that separates from the spermaceti is particularly fine and was used to keep machines running smoothly.

People who care about whales point out that men can find substitutes for these products. Sperm Whales, they say, must not be hunted from the seas!

PYGMY SPERM WHALE

PYGMY SPERM WHALE

A miniature of the giant Sperm Whale is to be found mainly in mild or warm tropical waters all around the world. This 13-foot "midget" is called the Pygmy Sperm Whale.

It may migrate to colder waters in the summer in search of fish for food. Pgymy Sperm Whales have been found in European waters, on both coasts of North America, and near New Zealand and Australia as well. Their small size has generally protected them from being hounded by hunters, who find the larger Sperms more profitable.

BAIRD'S BEAKED WHALE

BOTTLENOSE WHALE

CUVIER'S BEAKED WHALE

Beaked Whales

The Beaked Whales live out in mid-ocean, where the tasty squid are to be found. Squid, it seems, provide most of their meals. Men do not know a great deal about this family, because even the scientists who study whales have seen very few Beaked Whales.

Generally members of this family have long, narrow snouts, or "beaks." They have very few teeth; just one or two on each side in the lower jaw, and these sometimes poke out like small tusks.

The giant of the family is known as Baird's Beaked Whale. It grows to 42 feet in length. Most beaked whales range between 15 and 30 feet. The Bottlenose gets to be about 30 feet long, and its cousin known as Cuvier's Beaked Whale grows to be about 26 feet.

Cuvier's Whale is rarely seen, though it is believed that it lives in all oceans. It is unusual in color, so if you should happen by chance to see one, you should be able to recognize it. Most whales have dark gray backs and pale bellies. Cuvier's instead has a light back and a dark gray belly. And two small tusk-teeth poke up outside the mouth of the male.

Bottlenose is even more of an oddity. You may possibly see one traveling in a small school of ten or twelve whales in the North Atlantic, searching for squid to eat. Bottlenose is grayish black in color when it is young and becomes paler and yellowish as it grows older. It has a short beak that reminds some people of the neck of a bottle, and a high, bulging forehead. It also has a small fin that slopes backward, set far back toward its tail.

40

The White Whales

Beluga, the White Whale, usually lives in icy Arctic waters, in a world of white snowcaps and glittering green-white icebergs. There White Whale, like Polar Bear and Arctic Fox, finds a pale coat a protection.

As a calf, Beluga is dark gray. This color fades to dull yellow and later to white before the whale is full-grown. The pale skin is sometimes used as leather. When Beluga is full-grown it is about 14 feet long, so it is not likely to be confused with yellow-white Bottlenose, which is more than twice that length. And, unlike Bottlenose, Beluga has a round face and forehead and a bulging middle.

Schools of Belugas are usually very large. Often hundreds of these White Whales travel together. They call to one another as they swim. And they use a wide variety of whistles, clacks, squeaks, and birdlike sounds. Some of these calls are so musical that White Whales have sometimes been called "sea canaries."

Some of them like to explore icy northern rivers, like those of Siberia. Their strange musical calls have been heard many miles from the sea.

Beluga has a pale-skinned Arctic cousin. Its name is Narwhal, sometimes spelled Narwhale. You would have no trouble telling Beluga and Narwhal apart, though they belong to the same family. Narwhal is likely to be a few feet longer than Beluga, although that might be a bit difficult to judge if you saw one from a ship. Narwhal's coat is more grayish white, and it is spotted along the back. The best way to recognize Narwhal, though—a male, at least—is by its long, twisted tusk.

This ivory tusk starts out as a left upper tooth. But it grows through the whale's upper lip and extends out in front of its nose for six to ten feet! No wonder Narwhal is sometimes called "the unicorn of the sea." Its long, straight tusk of ivory is beautifully ornamented with grooves that spiral around it. It is the real-life version of the slender single horn on the forehead of the fairy-tale unicorn.

Once in a great while, a right upper tooth also pokes through, to form a pair of tusks. But usually the right upper tooth of a male Narwhal, like both teeth of the female, stays hidden in the jaw.

A few years ago a baby Narwhal that had lost its mother snuggled up to a canoe's smooth side for comfort. The boatmen rescued the baby, which would have starved if it had been left to take care of itself. Soon it was far from its Arctic birthplace, in a new home in a big-city aquarium. It is perhaps the only Narwhal to live among men.

BELUGA WHALES (Mother and baby)

NARWHAL

COMMON PORPOISE

BOTTLENOSE DOLPHIN

Ocean Dolphins

The family of Ocean Dolphins includes some whales and most dolphins and porpoises. The names "dolphin" and "porpoise" are both used to refer to the smaller members of the Ocean Dolphin family. But there are some differences between them. Usually porpoises have blunt noses and teeth shaped like lollipops. Most dolphins have long, thin snouts and cone-shaped teeth. But dolphins and porpoises are more like each other than the rest of their large family, which includes the powerful, 30-foot Killer Whale.

HERE COME THE KILLERS!

Through the water comes the throb of a measured beat. It is something like the sound of an army of marching feet on land. And like the approach of an enemy land army or a flight of warplanes, it frightens all who hear it. Mother whales and their babies dive to the bottom and lie motionless in hollows among the sea-bed rocks. Fish scurry away with a flurry of fins. For that drumbeat sound is a warning of the approach of a school of Killer Whales.

Killer Whales are the largest of the Ocean Dolphins. The males may grow to be 30 feet long.

Killers like to travel in a pack with others of their kind. Together, moving in perfect rhythm, they hunt other whales, seals, and otters. In the Antarctic they even hunt penguins for food. Let's see how they do it.

Here comes a big ice cake that has broken away from shore. A penguin strolls on the floating ice, waddling on its wide, flat feet. A bull seal nearby lifts its heavy shoulders. It peers down from the floe, scanning the water for fish. Neither of them sees the six-foot-high, triangular fin of Killer Whale cutting the surface of the sea on the far side of the floe. But the whale has seen them.

It blows out its breath in a fountain of spray. Then it inhales deeply and dives. It comes up under the near edge of the ice cake, shoving with all the power in its huge back. The ice rises. Its surface tilts at a sharp angle. The surprised penguin and the bull seal slide down into the water on the far side of the floe. The Killer pounces!

Creatures swimming in the water are usually warned of the approach of Killer Whales by the frightful pulse of sound. They try to hide. But the echoes of their flight ripple back to the Killer pack. These echoes help the huge hunters to locate their prey.

Fish make up most of the ordinary daily diet of Killer Whales. But the Killers are fierce hunters. Their sharp, slanting teeth can tear chunks of flesh from a seal or a walrus. A pack of them will attack even the largest whale, if it is separated from its friends. An angry Sperm Whale might knock out a Killer Whale with a smash of its wide tail or a slash of its big

A hungry Killer Whale tosses
an unsuspecting penguin and
a bull seal into the sea for
his next meal.

jaw. But very few other creatures can defend themselves against a pack of Killer Whales. In addition, the Killers are so swift and so clever that they are difficult for whale hunters to catch.

A few Killers have been captured by men and taken to aquariums. At first people were afraid to put a Killer into a tank with a smaller dolphin. Surely, men thought, this fierce fellow would kill the dolphin.

The Killer Whales put the men to shame. Some men, you know, like to kill animals just for sport. But this fiercest hunter of the seas kills only when it is hungry. In the aquarium it was well fed every day. It did not have to hunt in order to eat. So it became peaceable and friendly. As an experiment, a smaller dolphin and a Killer Whale were put into the same tank. Everyone was surprised to see that they got along very well. The Killer would even try to protect the small dolphin when it seemed to need help.

Captive Killer Whales have been equally friendly and gentle with people. A Killer will roll over and let a keeper feed it fish by hand. It will let a swimmer ride on its back. It likes to play ball with people, bouncing the ball from its nose.

These whales seem to enjoy learning and performing tricks, when they don't have to spend their time and energy hunting for food.

A well-fed Killer Whale in captivity becomes a good friend to the small dolphins in the same aquarium.

PYGMY KILLER

Once in a great while someone sights a Pygmy Killer Whale. Usually the sighting is off Japan or the west coast of Africa. The Pygmy is only about seven feet long when full grown and is rarely seen. It very closely resembles the giant Killer in everything but size.

PYGMY KILLER

FALSE KILLER

The smaller False Killer Whale lacks the towering back fin of the real Killer. False Killer does have a fin, but it is a relatively small one. It curves back in a hook rather than rising straight up. Some real Killer Whales have this type of curved fin, too. False Killer does not have the white belly and other sharp white markings of real Killers. Instead it is solid dark gray, with only occasional white, star-shaped markings. Otherwise its form is much like Killer's. But False Killer seldom grows to much more than 18 feet in length.

Like its bigger cousin, False Killer likes to travel in large groups. Usually these groups stay in the open sea. Now and then a group wanders so close to shore that in panic the whales may be grounded on the beach. Even when it is clear that the leaders of the pack are in trouble, the rest stay with them.

FALSE KILLER

45

PILOT WHALES

"That blackfish!" men of the windblown islands off the Scottish coast used to say of the Pilot Whale. "You can drive him like cattle!"

These islanders used the word "ca" for "drive." So they came to call the Pilot Whale "the caaing whale" as well as "blackfish."

For hundreds of years, the men of the islands, and seamen of other lands too, went out in their small boats to drive Pilot Whales ashore by the hundreds.

Pilot Whales, like the False Killer Whales, prefer to travel in very large groups. Sometimes a whole school of them travel close to a beach. They may ground themselves, or they can be driven by boatmen onto the sands, from which they cannot escape.

Pilot Whales winter in temperate waters. In spring they travel toward cooler waters, but not too far north or south. They go chasing their favorite food, the squid.

Some kinds of whales always follow the same course in migrating. Not the Pilots. They will go wherever their echo system tells them they can find a feast. Sometimes it seems that their echo system goes wrong. Then they pile up on some beach by the dozens.

A whale cannot live long without water to help support its weight and keep its skin cool. Going aground means the end of life's road. But for the men who find these whales, it means a rich haul in meat and blubber to boil down for oil.

"It'll be blackfish," men will say, when word comes of a grounding. Or, "Pilot Whales, no doubt." They scarcely need a glimpse of the big, dark bodies, 20 to 22 feet long. They do not need to check the long, pointed flippers and the bulging foreheads whalers call "melons" to be sure that they have come upon a school of grounded Pilot Whales.

THE FRIENDLY DOLPHINS

The sun shines on warm beach sand and blue sea. Children, and some of their parents, are leaping in the white froth of the surf, swimming, and shouting for joy.

Out beyond the breakers, another family group appears. They also are enjoying the sunny day. This is a family of dolphins, playing as happily as any of the humans. They play follow-the-leader across the waves, leaping high out of the water in graceful arcs.

Now, one leaves the line and bounds in toward the beach. A girl leaves her playmates and swims to meet the dolphin. Soon, seated on its broad, curving back, she waves to her friends as her sleek mount streaks through the waters.

This playful and friendly creature belongs to one of the whale groups called Common Dolphins. The name does not seem quite accurate, for this is one of the most distinctive dolphins to be found. It wears a black mask outlined in white around its eyes and handsome stripes of brown, yellow, and white beneath its black back "cloak." It is rather slender and elegant in shape and has a nicely pointed back fin. Its beak is long and toothy. And when Common Dolphin leaps and dives in rhythm with its friends, the whole team is as graceful as a group of ballet dancers.

It is not surprising to learn that 2,500, even 3,500, years ago artists delighted in painting dolphins on palace walls. People of Greece and Crete decorated jugs and bowls and vases, even coins, with dolphin forms. Sculptors modeled dolphins in clay and had the figures cast in bronze. Other artists pictured dolphins in mosaic floors, made by fitting together many small pieces of colored stone. Sometimes they showed a dolphin with a boy riding on its back.

There are many very old stories about the friendship between youngsters and dolphins that have come down to us through the years. For a long time, people thought these tales were just pleasant make-believe. But in modern times several dolphins have become famous for their friendliness to people.

47

One of the most famous appeared in a bay outside a New Zealand harbor almost a hundred years ago. He was medium-size—12 feet is medium-size for a dolphin. He was flat-faced and gray, one of the sort called Risso's Dolphin. For years he kept watch over the ships that came and went in his bay. He followed every steamer, leaping and diving and sporting about. This delighted all the passengers. Soon people were coming to the harbor just to see the dolphin, who was named Pelorus Jack. He became so famous that the legislature passed a law to protect him.

Another dolphin, a female, began to play with the children in the shallow water off another New Zealand beach about twenty years ago. She would bob up close in front of the children and let them pat her. She learned to play ball with them. She would toss a beach ball into the air with her nose. Then she would spin about and swat it with her tail.

She would also swim between a child's legs and let the child ride on her back. Stories like this are told of children thousands of miles apart—and thousands of years apart in time.

Other pleasant reports have come in. A man who was in danger of drowning was saved by dolphins that held him up until he was rescued. A woman swimming alone was caught in an undertow and was being carried out to sea. She floundered, unable to reach the surface. Then she felt something lift her up. Soon she found herself on a sandy beach. The first person who came to help her said that as a wave carried her up onto the sand, he saw a dolphin swim away.

These rescue stories are not hard to believe. Whales of many varieties have been seen supporting their babies with their flippers. A person is smaller than a baby whale. And these sea mammals have a good deal of intelligence. They can do more than use their skills to help themselves and their babies. They can figure out how to work—and play—in new and unfamiliar ways.

Mother dolphins, like all whale mothers, are very watchful and affectionate. A mother does not like to be more than ten feet or so from her young baby. If she rests, she may close her far eye, but the one nearer the baby stays open. When she swims, she makes certain that the baby is close. The calf beats its small tail as fast as it can, to keep up with its mother's speed. Its swimming may be a little wobbly at first, but the mother dolphin does not mind.

At nap time, the mother floats just below the surface, often with her blowhole in the air. To stay there, she must keep her tail moving gently. And close to the mother's tail, the baby sleeps, rising to breathe whenever its mother does.

When the baby wants some milk, the mother dolphin pushes the milk out into its mouth so it can gulp it down quickly and be ready to breathe. When a dolphin baby is small, it takes a little milk about every twenty minutes. By the time it is six months old, the baby starts learning to eat fish. Soon the youngster will need 18 or 20 pounds of fish a day

to satisfy it. The dolphin catches each fish in strong, sharp teeth, flips it around, and swallows it whole.

Swimming down near the rocky sea bottom one day, a young dolphin chases an eel. (This is a true story; people were watching.) Dolphin knows Eel is good to eat. This time the snakelike sea creature manages to hide in a narrow space between two rocks. Young Dolphin pokes at Eel, but Eel stays where it is safe.

With a flip of its tail, Dolphin swims away. Soon Dolphin spots a spiny-backed Scorpion Fish. Dolphin pounces on Scorpion Fish and catches it. But it does not swallow this prickly mouthful.

With Scorpion Fish held carefully in its mouth, Dolphin goes back to the rocks, where Eel still hides. There it pokes at Eel with the prickly, stinging spines on Scorpion Fish's back. Eel cannot stand much of that stinging, and is forced to wriggle out of the shelter. Then Dolphin drops Scorpion Fish and darts away after the tastier Eel.

Dolphin and its friends not only learn how to do things like catching fish for food. They learn how to solve problems, like getting Eel to come out from hiding. And young Dolphin used Scorpion Fish very much as a person would use a tool. That takes thinking.

Dolphin uses a Scorpion Fish to force Eel out of hiding.

Dolphins certainly seem able to think well. Those that have been captured by men learn how to play games with people. But they do more than that. They learn to make up new games of their own. And if a person stops playing with them, they grunt their annoyance.

Dolphins are just as playful among themselves. They play by gently bumping noses and snouts, and by rolling over in the water. A young dolphin likes to play and swim with good friends. If it is separated from its dolphin friends, it seems sad. And it is happy to see them again after they have been apart.

Dolphins have no trouble telling one another how they feel. Common Dolphin whistles through its blowhole, which is shaped like a small new moon. It often uses whistling sounds at play. It clicks out sounds when it wants to locate things from the echoes—as larger whales do. And if it is annoyed, it may clap its jaws together loudly. It has so many sounds with which to express its feelings that men still hope they may some day learn to understand dolphin talk.

Radio music attracts Common Dolphin. At night, when the dark sea glows with strange light, it may come swimming around a small boat where a radio is playing. It may nuzzle the boat with its nose to show that it wants to be friends. Turn off the radio, and chances are that Dolphin will leave. It will leap away with water drops flying like diamonds from its fin and tail.

Dolphins seem to listen closely to human voices as well as to music. Men of some of the South Sea islands have special dolphin calls. When their people need to catch a dolphin or two, these men cup their hands and send a special call ringing out over the sea. Soon, sure enough, a dolphin appears. And sometimes a friendly dolphin seems to imitate a human voice or laugh.

Men have tested dolphins by throwing them two fish at a time. One is large, the other smaller. The dolphin always chooses the larger one. It can tell the difference even on the darkest night, thanks to its sonar. A dolphin can also identify a fine fish net in the dark by sound waves alone. A very coarse net does not send back as many sound waves as a fine net, so Dolphin may not know it is there and may be caught in it. But usually its sonar echo system works as well as any that men have so far been able to build.

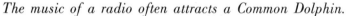

The music of a radio often attracts a Common Dolphin.

GOOD-NATURED BOTTLENOSE AND OTHER OCEAN DOLPHINS

The aquarium show is ending. Killer Whale has jumped twenty feet into the air for a fish held in its trainer's hand. Bottlenose Dolphin has done its graceful dance and bounced a ball on its nose. Now Bottlenose bows, with a wave of its flippers, and seems to smile at the people gathered to watch the show. Its "smile" may be just the natural curve of its long mouth. But its good humor is real.

Bottlenose, who shares its name with one of the larger Beaked Whales, is probably the best known of all dolphins. Have you ever seen a show of trained dolphins in an aquarium in the United States or in Japan, Australia, or the Netherlands? If so, you have probably seen Bottlenose doing its tricks.

Tursiops truncatus is its scientific name. Several kinds of dolphins are called *Tursiops,* after a big fish they resemble. One of these is Bottlenose. Another is the dolphin nicknamed Cowfish.

There are many Ocean Dolphins. There is the Spinner, which likes to leap playfully several feet out of the water. There it spins around several times before falling back. There are the Speckled, the Spotted, and the Borneo White Dolphins. But none has come to live so happily with man as Bottlenose.

Bottlenose Dolphins have been carried to many aquariums from their home in the Atlantic. Usually a whale travels on a bed of water-soaked plastic foam and is covered with wet rubber blankets or splashed with water to keep its skin cool and damp. On this spongy wet bed the whale can travel quite comfortably by ship or even by airplane.

Some larger whales seem to be upset by being captured. So does the Common Porpoise. Men have a hard time getting this dolphin to an aquarium in good health. If it does arrive safely, it must be persuaded to eat. It usually refuses fish and even squid.

It would be even harder to provide a diet of plankton for a full-grown Baleen or Whalebone Whale. And most of them are so large that it would be hard to build a tank large enough for one to swim in. So men have not figured out a way to keep these giants to adulthood, where people can watch them and learn more about them.

Cheerful Bottlenose Dolphin does not seem to be concerned or fearful about being captured. It eats well and likes to learn new tricks. No one who has seen Bottlenose in action will forget its graceful flights through the air, and its merry smile.

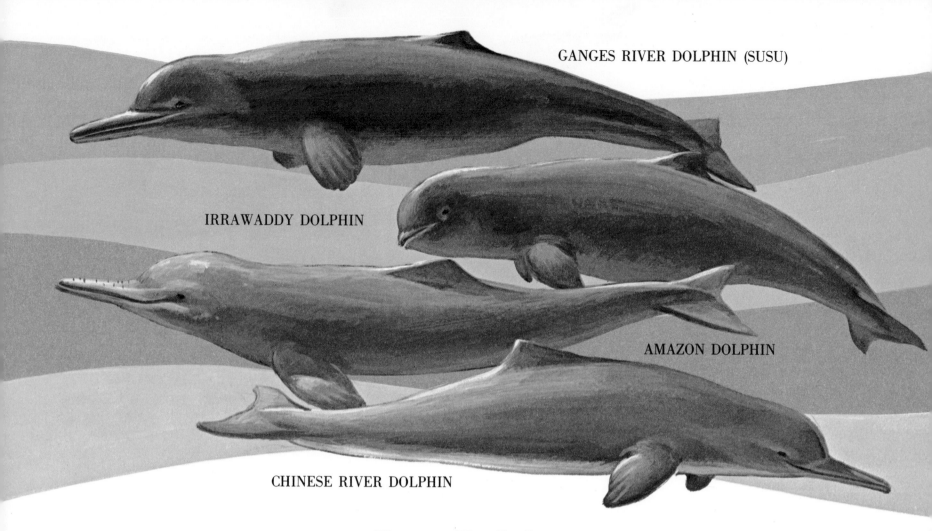

GANGES RIVER DOLPHIN (SUSU)

IRRAWADDY DOLPHIN

AMAZON DOLPHIN

CHINESE RIVER DOLPHIN

River Dolphins

The smallest of all the whale relatives are the dolphins that live in rivers. Some belong to the Ocean Dolphin family. They venture out from the shelter of rivers into nearby waters of salty seas. Others belong to the Freshwater Dolphin family. All dolphins, of course, are Toothed Whales.

Some scientists think that these dolphins, like seals and walruses, have not quite completed the ages-long move back to the water. Some River Dolphins still have a suggestion of neck. Their heads are not completely streamlined. Their tail flukes are not as wide as those that help larger whales swim rapidly through the seas. Wide tail flukes also help whales in diving and rising to the surface. This skill is not so important to small dolphins living in shallow rivers.

River Dolphins still have "fingers" visible in their flippers. And some still have a little hair left from the ages when they were land animals. They must breathe more frequently than seagoing whales.

Most River Dolphins range from 5 to 8 feet in length. Most have long, narrow jaws, lined with many teeth. They are found in widely separated rivers, such as the Amazon in Brazil, the Yangtze in China, the Ganges in India, and La Plata in Uruguay. Almost every river has a slightly different variety of dolphin.

One variety, a dull-black dolphin, lives in the Ganges, Indus, and Brahmaputra rivers of South Asia. People of India call this dolphin *Susu*. It wallows along in the mud of the river bottom, often swimming on its side or back. There it snaps at food with the many teeth in its long, sharp beak. But it cannot really see what it is snapping at, because its small eyes are almost useless in the muddy water.

Another dolphin often makes its home in the Irrawaddy River in Burma and is named the Irrawaddy Dolphin for this river. But it may also be found in the Mekong River of Southeast Asia and in the nearby waters off the coast. It grows to be about 7 feet long and is dark gray in color. It has a bulgy forehead and a small mouth in place of the long beak most River Dolphins have.

China's dolphin is found only in one lake, hundreds

of miles up the Yangtze River. It is a rather pale gray on top and a still lighter shade below. Like India's Susu, it is almost blind.

Off the southern coast of China, there is a dolphin that is nearly white. Other relatives, some speckled, some gray, swim the warm waters of the Indian Ocean and the South China Sea.

South America has at least four varieties of River Dolphins. The Guiana River Dolphin sometimes ventures out into the salt water of the Caribbean Sea. Another salt-water variety also lives in the Rio de Janeiro harbor.

A true Freshwater Dolphin roams the vast Amazon and Orinoco River systems. If you should see one, you might be surprised to find short bristles growing on the top of Amazon Dolphin's beak. Some scientists think that these hairs may help the dolphin "feel" its way through mud-clouded shallow waters. Others think that the hairs may be left over from the time long ago when dolphins and whales were hairy-coated land animals. Amazon Dolphin grows to no more than 7 feet, which is small for the order of whales. But the river people, who call it *bouto*, or *bufeo*, consider it sacred.

Smallest of all dolphins is the one that swims in South America's Rio la Plata and the nearby offshore waters, farther south than the Amazon. This little dolphin, with its long beak and sharp teeth, is a good fish-catcher.

Some members of the large and varied Ocean Dolphin family are not much bigger. The Common or Harbor Porpoise seldom grows to be more than 5 or 6 feet long. It is black backed and white bellied. It likes medium warm waters and often swims far up rivers. This small porpoise might be surprised to learn that it is related to the 60-foot giant of the sea, the mighty Sperm Whale.

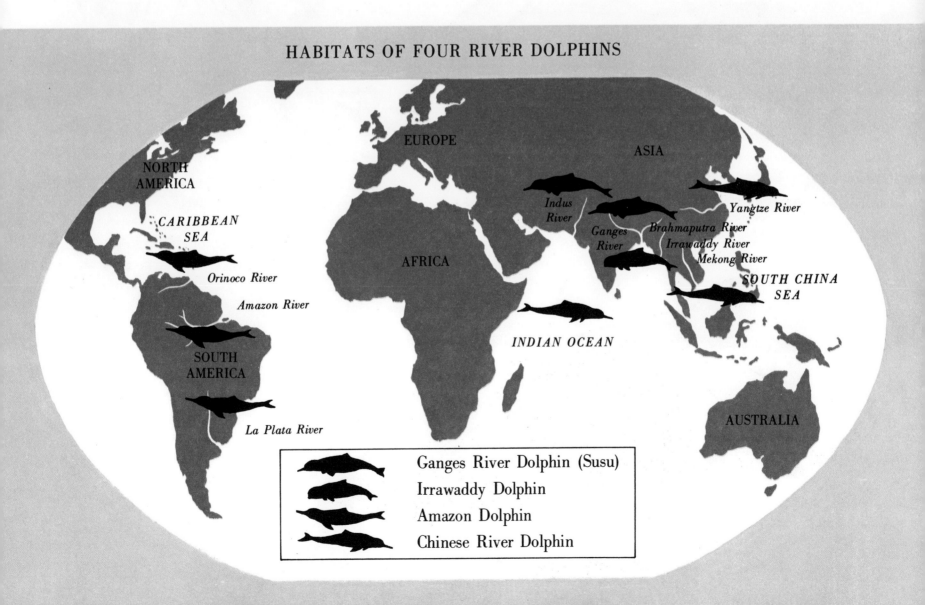

HABITATS OF FOUR RIVER DOLPHINS

EUROPE

ASIA

NORTH AMERICA

CARIBBEAN SEA

Indus River

Ganges River

Brahmaputra River

Irrawaddy River

Mekong River

Yangtze River

Orinoco River

AFRICA

SOUTH CHINA SEA

Amazon River

SOUTH AMERICA

INDIAN OCEAN

La Plata River

AUSTRALIA

Ganges River Dolphin (Susu)
Irrawaddy Dolphin
Amazon Dolphin
Chinese River Dolphin

Whales and Men

The waters of the North Atlantic toss angrily under lead-gray skies. Long stretches of its coast rise in rocky cliffs. Several thousand years ago, small boats pushed out into the open sea from coves and inlets in those shores. Sturdy boatmen lowered nets into the water to catch the fish that swam there in huge schools. And now and then they encountered a "Monster of the Deep." Today we call such "monsters" whales.

Wild tales were told of these sea giants. One was the story of a great storm at sea in Bible times. To quiet the waves, the seamen threw overboard a passenger named Jonah, who had displeased his God. Jonah, the story claimed, was swallowed by "a great fish." After three days and nights, he was spat up, still in good health, onto dry land.

There were other whale tales. Long ago, people thought the earth was flat. They believed that all around the lands rolled the vast Ocean Sea. People of Mediterranean lands thought that if a ship sailed out through the Gates of Hercules (now called the Strait of Gibraltar) it would surely be swallowed by huge sea monsters that lived in the wild waters beyond.

The Norsemen of long ago did sail that Ocean Sea. So at least some of them really knew about those sea giants, the whales. And not all they knew was bad. Now and then a whale was washed ashore. Villagers learned that whale meat was good to eat. They learned that the whales' thick layer of fat was full of useful oil. Their craftsmen learned to make tools from the whales' big, strong bones.

People grew tired of waiting for the waves to toss an occasional stray whale up on the beach. So they set up watchtowers along the seacoasts. There watchers kept a lookout for whales. When one was sighted, a bell was rung. Men ran to their boats and put out to sea. With noise and splashing, they tried to drive the whales in toward the beach, where they would be helpless and easily killed.

After some time, men became bolder. They fastened sharp, barbed heads to their throwing spears. They called these *harpoons*. They threw these weapons at the whales out in open water. But a whale could swim away and dive into the depths with a harpoon in its body. So the hunters learned to fasten long lines to their spears.

This was a risk for the hunters. A whale wounded by a harpoon and still attached to the line could drag a boat after it. Often the whalers had to cut their lines to keep from being dragged down into the sea by a diving whale. Many boats were smashed to bits by the slam of a whale's broad tail. There was a good deal of truth to the old tales about the dangers of the Ocean Sea!

It was not only Norsemen who learned these lessons. Eskimos of the Arctic paddled their small skin canoes out among the towering, floating ice mountains. They hunted whales and other mammals of the sea uncounted years ago. Villagers on the coasts of France, Holland, England, Russia, and Japan also hunted whales hundreds of years ago.

Early European hunters chased the easily driven bands of small whales onto beaches. They harpooned the larger whales. Japanese hunters used harpoons and also large nets. The crews of two Japanese boats would spread a net between them across the path of a whale. Then the men of the other boats of the fleet would set up a terrific noise with sticks. This usually frightened the whale into swimming ahead until it was trapped by the net. Then, when the men threw their harpoons, the whale did not have a chance to get away.

The dead whale was dragged ashore by the boatmen. There a "factory," or "try works," had been set up on the beach. These factories differed from country to country. But they all had much the same equipment.

The coopers had to have wood for shaping barrels for whale oil. The smiths had to have fire and tools for sharpening harpoons. The meat-curers had to have salt and racks for processing the whale meat. There had to be storage space for the horny whalebone from the Baleen Whales and for the skeletons of all the catch. And there were stacks of firewood, coils of rope, and kitchens for feeding the workers. A factory was a busy place when a whale was brought in. And there was no time to waste.

First came the "cutting in," or "flensing." This was the process of peeling off the thick blanket of blubber. Special tools such as flensing knives and eight-foot blubber forks were used. In some factories the dead whale was roped up. Crews of men twisted big cranks to turn winches. The winches pulled ropes. And the ropes turned the whale around and around as the blubber was peeled off in long, spiral strips.

Then the blubber was cut into chunks. Fires were built under huge try pots. And the chunks of blubber were tossed into the pots. As the fat melted, or was "tried out," it sent up thick clouds of black smoke —and a strong smell!

The pots were soon half filled with clear, amber-colored oil. Crisp lumps of "cracklings" floated on the oil. These lumps were scooped out, and the oil, when it cooled, was poured into barrels. Then the workers felt that one big part of their work was done.

Whale oil kept the lamps burning in countless homes in the days before electricity was widely used.

If the catch was a Sperm Whale, the huge head was cut off. Then a hole was cut in the skull case, and the clear spermaceti was dipped out in buckets. As the liquid hardened to wax, it provided the makings for excellent, sweet-smelling candles.

When the catch was a Baleen Whale, the horny lengths of whalebone were one of the most valuable products. The base of the "moustache" of horny whalebone was cut out from inside the skull as a block. The strong, springy strips made umbrella ribs,

hoops for ladies' hoopskirts, and handles for gentlemen's riding whips. Some of the whalebone was woven into chair seats or bedsprings. The coarse fibers along the frayed edges of the whalebone even made plumes for soldiers' helmets! Hunters were glad to find a whale with a good mouthful of whalebone.

The next step was the "leaning up." Men cut the meat off the huge bones of the whale at this time. Not all the people who hunted whales liked the taste of whale meat, but many did, particularly the Japanese. Some ground the meat for animal food.

Most of the bones were sawed and chopped into bits—especially in Japan. The bone chunks were boiled in salt water. Then the oil that rose to the top was skimmed off, and the water drained away. The chunks that remained were ground into bone meal to be used as fertilizer.

Some whalers used bones, particularly the huge jawbones, in building huts or for gates or fences. And, of course, they knocked the big teeth out of the jawbones.

Whales' teeth were valuable as trade goods. Villagers on South Sea islands, such as Tonga, where whalers often stopped, liked whales' teeth better than any other ornaments. They were glad to trade fruits, chickens, wood, or other supplies for a single cone-shaped tooth.

In the 1600s, large whaling ships began to sail the seas. Men continued to chase the whales in small boats that were lowered over the sides of the big ships. But instead of dragging the catch to shore, they hauled it to shipside. There they fastened the huge body to the side of the ship with ropes. Men climbed down rope ladders to strip off the blubber.

Some ships packed the chunks of blubber in vats and carried it—a smelly cargo—until they reached the

A busy "try works" processes a captured whale. At left (A) is a capstan or winch used to pull the whale ashore and into position so the men can work on it. At top (B) men are "flensing"—removing the thick layer of blubber. Men at try pots (C) boil the blubber down into oil. At center (D) coopers are building barrels in which to transport the oil. After the blubber is cut off, the meat is removed from the bones, then salted and packed for shipment.

shore. On other ships crews set up try pots on the decks and boiled the blubber there.

Many sailors liked to carve the big whale teeth into small objects. Carving helped them to while away the many long, slow shipboard hours when their other work was done. Dominoes, penholders, tools for shaping piecrusts, and small animals carved from whale teeth were favorite items. Other men scratched and painted tiny pictures on the smooth surface of the ivory. This art of the sailors on old-time whaling ships came to be called *scrimshaw.*

Once large ships started to sail the open seas, whales far out at sea were not much safer than those close to shore. But the hunt was not safe for the whalers, either. Many boats were smashed by the battering nose or flailing tail of an injured whale. The whales still had a fair chance in the struggle.

Men developed more powerful weapons, though, as time went on. They began to shoot their harpoons or lances from guns. These guns gave men a great advantage over the whales. The whalers no longer had to depend on their own strength.

By the mid-1800s, more and more whalers were going to sea. Their voyages were longer and longer. Early whalers had rowed out from shore and back the same day, or the next. The first whaling ships had stayed at sea only a few weeks at a time. Later sailing ships often were away from home for two or three years at a time. Some voyages dragged on through four or five years. Every ship wanted to come home with its hold filled with casks of oil. The United States alone had 750 ships out hunting whales. Forty thousand American sailors were pursuing the giants of the deep.

There were whales in plenty during those lively years. How splendid it would have been if all the whalers had worked and planned together to limit the catch each year. Then there would have been enough whales to provide many, many people with a steady

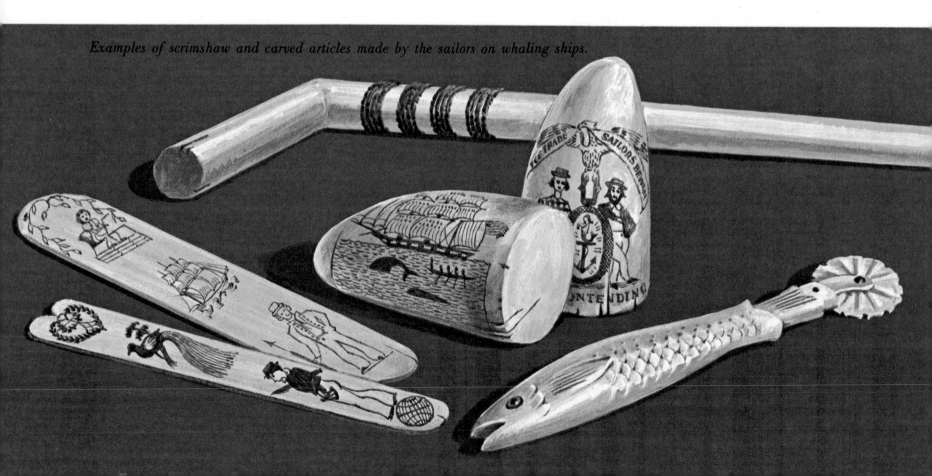

Examples of scrimshaw and carved articles made by the sailors on whaling ships.

A floating factory ship. A whale is being hauled aboard through a slipway in the stern. Another has already been pulled up a ramp to the deck for flensing and leaning up. The try pots and equipment for packing and storing are below deck.

supply of oil, meat, and bone, indefinitely. But no crew saw any reason why it should not catch as many whales as possible, as fast as possible. Surely no one worried about the future of the whales!

Gradually the Bowheads, with their very long whalebones, became scarce. The Sperm Whales, with their skull cases full of rich oil, became harder and harder to find. The slow-moving Humpbacks, the huge Blues, and the Grays became rare sights on the seas.

Still the whalers did not realize that they were hunting themselves out of jobs. Instead they built larger and larger ships, armed with more and more powerful weapons. Their new, swift, steam-powered ships could complete a long voyage in a season.

The first real "factory ship" was launched in 1925. It was so large that a whale could be hauled onto the deck for processing. There were other changes in whaling as time passed. Early whaling ships had kept a man on watch in a barrel-like crow's-nest high on the mast. Later, helicopters were sent out to spot swimming whales.

The whales no longer had a fair chance of escaping these hunters, with their swift ships, flying scouts, and cannons. The sleek, intelligent giants of the sea were being killed by tens of thousands each year.

At last men realized that these magnificent creatures soon would not exist any more unless something was done. Groups of men from many lands began to make rules to limit whale hunting. At first they set up limits on the regions of the seas where whaling ships could operate. That helped some varieties to survive.

In 1972, a ten-year ban on all whaling was decided upon. But a few countries would not agree to it. They had huge factory ships and large crews of sailors who had been trained to hunt whales for a living. They insisted that it was their right to catch as many whales as they could.

All the whale-hunting peoples of the world must agree if the ban is to succeed. And surely it must succeed! For it would be tragic if these splendid, intelligent, sociable creatures were to be wiped out because of man's greed.

If they are to survive, whales must have some years in which to travel the seas again and raise their babies in peace. Otherwise, young people of tomorrow may never have a chance to see a dolphin leap or a whale spout, or to hear the exciting call, "Thar she blows!" Unless firm action is taken soon, the glorious whales, including the largest living beings of all times, may vanish forever from the waters of the earth.

INDEX

60

61

BCDE

Cuvier's Beaked Whale
26 feet

Killer Whale
30 feet

Beluga Whale
14 feet

Right Whale
50 feet

Sperm Whale
60 feet